TICKNER'S LIGHT HORSE

TICKNER'S
LIGHT HORSE

WRITTEN AND ILLUSTRATED
by

John Tickner

°THE°
SPORTSMAN'S
PRESS
LONDON

First published 1956
Reprinted by The Sportsman's Press in 1988

© *John Tickner* 1988

British Library Cataloguing in Publication Data
Tickner, John, *1913–*
   Tickner's light horse.
   1. Livestock: Horses. Riding – Humour
   I. Title
   798.2′3′0207

ISBN 0-948253-25-8

Printed in Great Britain at The Bath Press, Avon

CONTENTS

' 'Eavens, wot a lot of rubbish 'as
been written about 'osses.'

R. S. SURTEES, 1803–1864

INTRODUCTION

According to statistics, there are more light horses about today than ever. This will be surprising to many people who have never ridden a horse, but then there are even more people about than horses.

Since man discovered that the shaggy wild creature who neighed instead of bellowed could be persuaded to pull sledges and carts, and even carry him about on it's back, he has regarded the horse as his second best friend, next to the dog.

Man also found that he could look extremely dignified when sitting on a horse's back, especially when talking to people on foot, and so riding became extremely popular. It has remained so, even though the motor car has made the horse non-essential as transport.

There is only one snag about being on horseback and that is that a really determined horse can, in a matter of seconds, transform one from looking dignified in the saddle to looking undignified on the ground.

Although this book was first published in 1956, I find no reason to alter it. Nothing has changed; horses often still get the last laugh, only more of them are doing so than ever before.

John Tickner
Westhide, Hereford

I

Your first Pony

The First Horse

EVER since the first man was kicked by the first horse a bond of friendship has existed between the species, even to the extent of man providing the horse with iron shoes with which it can kick him harder.

The first horse, we are told, was about the size of a fox, but man gradually grew larger horses, and this, although it probably caused considerable annoyance to foxes, undoubtedly made foxhunting more interesting and added to the excitement of falling off horses—and man has certainly been doing that ever since he domesticated the creatures. It is recorded that the Romans found the Ancient Britons using ferocious shaggy ponies which, drawing chariots

Native Ponies in Ancient Britain

with knives attached to the wheels, cleared lanes through the ranks of their astonished legions in no time at all. These were the ancestors of our native ponies, many of which accomplish the same feat among the ranks of adults in the hunting field today and do it, mark you, without the aid of chariots and knives.

In the Middle Ages, when man was wearing armour of considerable weight, a horse of larger and stronger build was required, and much the same type of animal is still used for hunting by middle-aged men weighing almost as much as their ancestors but without the armour. Getting into the saddle is more of an ordeal now than it was then, for a chair, furtively placed round the back of the barn, has replaced the pulley system which knights used unashamedly in public.

The Native Pony Today

After the questionable invention of gunpowder, the heavy horse, apart from its occasional use as mentioned above, was largely replaced for riding purposes by lighter horses which have achieved immortality in poems in which desperate characters desperately carry important messages; in sporting prints where, carrying sporting bloods, they can be seen jumping impossible obstacles; as race horses; as the chargers of famous generals at famous battles, and looking very unlikely as equestrian statues in city squares.

It should be mentioned that horses were used in vehicles before anyone had the nerve to sit on them and, throughout the ages, it was smart to be seen driving any number from one to four. To be seen driving four today is still considered pretty smart, but to be seen driving one is often regarded as rather odd—unless, of course, it is an expensive hackney in the show ring.

Despite threats that this is the mechanical age and that we shall all soon be off to the moon, there are still plenty of horses about. They are to be seen carrying bored-looking cavalrymen in musical rides and Trooping the Colour, at horse shows, races, the hunting field, Wimbledon Common, sometimes in Rotten Row and quite frequently pulling horseless carriages out of mud and snow.

How do you get a horse? As stealing one is considered to be an anti-social act even today, you are faced with buying one. Being given one is a doubtful blessing because the animal is usually either on its last three legs or downright dangerous, and frequently both.

We will consider your first pony. The first thing to do is to ask Father, and the intelligent time to do it is immediately after dinner. The best method is to lead up to the subject by asking him about his first day's hunting. He won't know that you know he was a shocking horseman, Mother having innocently given you this piece of news sometime before. You don't have to listen to his lengthy and highly imaginative account. Just wait until he pauses for breath and then tell him that all your little friends are having ponies because 'their parents can afford it'. This should do the trick.

Father will then mention casually at the club he visits before lunch at weekends that he is 'looking out for a pony for my daughter '. Even you will be amazed at the number of people who overhear this remark and know of a pony that has ' got too small for the present owner '. There is always the possibility that this will give Father the impression that ponies get smaller and smaller until they disappear.

A kind person who deals in horses will soon ring up and tell Father he has the very thing—persons who deal are as expert at finding telephone numbers as they are at finding ponies.

Early the next Saturday morning the dealer and a pony will be at the front door. The pony, and quite likely the dealer, will be so hairy that it may be quite a problem to tell which end is whose. But don't worry, they are wearing their winter coats and you will find out in the summer.

An Interesting Moment

Before he buys the pony, Father must see it trotted up and down and make appropriate and knowledgeable noises, the most usual of which are ' mm ' and ' ah '. He must then bend down and take hold of one of the pony's legs—this is always an interesting moment because there is a distinct possibility that the pony will take hold of Father's leg first.

Strictly speaking, you should then ride the pony at a walk, trot and canter round the paddock and put it over a small jump, but the dealer will probably point out that the ground is too hard, or possibly the pony needs to settle down first, or perhaps even that you might get dirty, or something equally thoughtful.

The next thing you know is that the pony is being turned into the paddock and Father is writing out a cheque. Of course, it won't happen quite like this if the dealer is one of the many famous and highly reputable ones. In that case the pony will indeed be put through all its paces and so will you and Father, before Father finds himself writing out an even larger cheque. Anyway, now you are a real pony owner and, as many of the lady writers on ponies might say, ' Golly, isn't it jolly !'

II

How to keep your first Pony

THE little beast is now in the paddock, peering through its mane to see what has bought it and probably making up its mind whether it shall reveal its true nature immediately or later on.

There are two recognised ways of keeping a pony. They are at grass or indoors—which, of course, means in a stable, not the house. The first essential for keeping a pony at grass is lots of grass. Care, however, should be taken not to turn a very small pony into a field of very tall grass, because this will make it exceedingly difficult to find the

Ambush

15

animal and also provide it with opportunities to lie up and ambush you while you are looking for it. It is also important to remember that horses and ponies will not eat just any old grass. The green luscious-looking stuff which almost makes your own mouth water is certain to be distasteful to the pony; whereas the short, yellowy-looking grass just the other side of the fence is equally certain to be to the pony what cream cakes are to its owner. It does not take an owner long to discover that, when the pony appears to be thinking quietly, it is often thinking how to get away from its own grass and get at the other grass.

In the winter you must give it all the hay it can eat— and it can eat a veritable haystack in a remarkably short time, a fact that will dismay Father even more than it astonishes you, for he will have to pay for it.

Keeping a pony in a loose box will mean a lot more work for you, because the average father certainly will not fall for the job of ' mucking out '. This somewhat crude expression means sweeping out the creature's bedroom daily, in

It can lie cosily at nights

Oats have a peculiar effect on some ponies

addition to which you will have to make its bed of straw so that it can lie cosily at nights, probably dreaming up what it will do to you when you get on its back.

Ponies living-in are often given oats as well as hay. Oats have a most peculiar effect on some ponies and are apt to send them slightly crazy. In fact, ponies that are allowed to stuff themselves with oats and are not exercised regularly are liable to wait for you to get into the saddle, count ten and go straight up in the air. You are certain to go even higher in the air, causing the pony to shriek with laughter.

It is, therefore, probably wiser to keep the pony out at grass. If you do this you will have to keep it in—in the paddock that is—for there is nothing in the world so clever at getting out of anywhere as a small and hairy pony.

You must walk all round the paddock, inspecting the fence to make sure there aren't any gaps. If there are not, you will feel that all is well and probably go and watch show-jumping on T.V. An hour later you go to have a look at the pony again. It isn't there, but there is a gap in the fence instead, for there is nothing in the world so clever at making gaps as a pony.

In the field of waving oats beyond the fence you find a long passageway of trampled stalks and at the end of the passage, smiling and stuffing itself, is the pony. You creep up, grab it and return it to the paddock, hoping the farmer will think the lane through the crop was made by dogs, hikers or wood pigeons on foot.

In this event, Father must be persuaded to spend all the next Saturday making the fence absolutely gap-proof. The pony will stand quietly, furtively watching the proceedings and thinking.

The next time you go to look at the pony, there is no pony, but there are also no gaps. It has jumped out, for nothing is so clever at jumping out as a pony. This time you retrieve it from the village where the policeman has found it apparently discussing the church bazaar with the Rector in the middle of the square.

Father spends all the next Saturday putting wire round the top of the fence of the paddock at a height that even a pony with White City ambitions is unlikely to attempt.

Having fixed the fencing, the next thing to do is to

make sure that the pony has an adequate shelter in the paddock, for even the hairiest ponies should have protection from the weather. When you have pointed this out to Father, he will be delighted to put one up for you. If it is winter, make sure, too, that he carries up bales of straw so that the pony has a deep and cosy retreat in which it can lie plotting. Once all this has been done, the pony will stay in the middle of the paddock, day and night, avoiding the shelter like the plague.

It is essential to get into the habit of catching the pony daily. You start by walking quietly towards it making affectionate noises. It will wait until you are just about to put your arm around its neck and then, with what sounds suspiciously like a snigger, will stroll away. You repeat this performance for three hours and then go to watch T.V., leaving the pony sniggering in the corner of the paddock.

The next time you attempt it, the pony will appear to be asleep. It will be difficult to be sure about this, because you will be unable to see its eyes through its mane. Just as you think you have got it, it will utter a scream of laughter and trot round you, just out of range, until you are pretty nearly dizzy.

The next approach must be made with sugar. Stretching out your hand gently and slowly, you offer the titbit to the pony. You will be lucky if you get away with all your fingers. The pony, munching its sugar and neighing happily, will treat you to a galloping performance all around the paddock.

The last resort is a rope. Collect all the adults you can, get one of them to tie one end of the rope to the fence and get the others to drive the pony into a corner. This should not take more than a day. Once the pony is in the corner, the rope should be taken swiftly and quietly right across, penning the pony in. In practice, the pony, grinning evilly, will make a dash for liberty, someone will get kicked and the rest will trip over the rope.

Most experts insist that to give up trying to catch the pony will be taken as a sign of weakness, but the writer advocates going to bed sometime.

At about 1 a.m. you will be awakened with the news that the little horror has been found in a garden four miles away. It crept out under the fence, for nothing is so clever at creeping under fences as a pony.

It is often claimed that ponies are not very bright but by this time you will have been made to think that ponies also think.

Crept out under the fence

III

Riding Schools

Throughout Britain there are numerous establishments which exist simply for two worthy reasons—to keep the standard of horsemanship high and to keep riding instructors in bread and butter and beer. These establishments, all called riding schools, vary in type from a couple of lean-to sheds full of small, fat and bored ponies who spend most of the week twiddling their hoofs and gossiping and only working at weekends, to the palatial building full of well-bred horses and pretty, well-bred girl grooms who never have time to gossip at all.

Between these extremes there is the middle-sized establishment with middle-bred horses tended by, perhaps, two middle-bred girls. At this type of riding school the fees charged for instruction are also middle-sized, and so it is reasonable to assume that the majority of learners will find it to their taste.

We will suppose you are a girl in your teens who, having been instructed on your first pony by a benevolent uncle for some time, are now well aware that you can ride but want to have a few expert lessons to 'polish up a bit'. You arrive at the riding stable looking very smart in a tight polo-necked sweater, well-cut, birthday-present breeches

Riding school cavalcade

and highly polished boots which, although they were Mother's, fit your shapely legs like a glove.

One of the girl-groom instructresses will take one look at you, point to a dopey-looking horse and say, 'That's yours—can you get on?' Slightly offended, you put one foot in the stirrup and give the most appalling exhibition of struggling on to a horse's back that you have ever done in your life.

The instructress will look a lot and say nothing and, leaving you pink in the face sitting in the middle of the yard on your horse, will bustle efficiently about, collecting an assortment of children, ponies, one middle-aged man and a horse together and, forming you all into a cavalcade, will lead you out of the yard on an obvious thoroughbred which makes the rest of the mounts look positively shabby. She will remain silent until you reach the wide open spaces when she will suddenly shout, 'Trot!' Turning in her saddle, she will stare at you hard, causing you to get completely out of rhythm with your horse which feels as though it has only three legs anyway.

The instructress will ask you if you have ever ridden before, raise her eyebrows sceptically at your reply and from then on proceed to prove that you are not a horsewoman. At the end of the ride, she remarks that by the time you have been going to the stables every weekend for three months (at at least ten bob a time) you will be getting the idea. You feel pretty sure you have already got the idea but, nevertheless, you will be seeing a lot of those stables.

Like members of every other profession, riding masters and riding mistresses may be placed in a few categories, with slight variation. There is the hearty horsey type. The man will probably have a weather-beaten face, a large moustache which looks as if it once belonged to the cavalry but probably never did, a too-loud waistcoat and a slightly bow-legged walk which he has cultivated for years and which makes him look as if he is a chronic sufferer from rickets. He will continually slap his whip on his boot and on yours, too, if you get too close.

The female in this category will look much the same as

Types of riding masters

the man but without the moustache, probably, and will have a somewhat louder voice. It is possible to put up with these types if you are only going to see them on Saturdays.

The second type is downright seedy, and here both the male and the female will be pretty much over-ripe versions of the first type. The moustache will droop, the waistcoat be somewhat soiled, the voice husky and there will be occasions when you doubt if it really was the weather that beat their faces into that complexion.

The third type is madly efficient. The man will be good-looking in a rugged way, smartly and absolutely correctly dressed from his bowler to his boots, and will appear to have served in a cavalry unit and probably has. The female of the species will be equally well turned-out and look as if she has hunted in the Shires and probably has. The standard of their instruction will be as high as their fees, their manners impeccable and altogether they will probably terrify you far more than their horses do.

The riding-school horses fit even more snugly into types. Nearly all of them are there to prove to you, and anyone else watching, that you cannot ride. A frequently-met type is the horse that won't go—not for you anyway. It is often quite a presentable beast and you are delighted when it is brought out. Once in the saddle, you pick up the reins and squeeze it with your legs. It may move one ear slightly back. You squeeze a bit harder, and the other ear twitches. It keeps this up until it has trapped you into banging both legs against its sides, whereupon the instructress, who has been waiting for this moment, is delighted to pounce upon you, give you a lecture and demonstration on the use of the aids, and suggest a few more weeks' lessons.

Another and even more cunning character is the horse that sets off with you willingly enough, striding out and convincing you that you are as much one with your horse

Won't Go

Goes to
Sleep

Won't Stop

Riding school horses

as a Centaur. A quarter of a mile from the stable the animal's head begins to droop, its pace becomes slower and you begin to wonder whether it will fall down. But it just gets slower and slower until it stops, and no amount of surreptitious squeezing or even furious banging will have any effect. Turn it around and point it stablewards and it wakes up, hurries home and puts you in the embarrassing position of having to explain that you have suddenly remembered an appointment and had to cut your ride short. You also have to think up some excuse for not having the brute next time.

The third type of riding-school beast is often, to your innocent eyes, a joy to look upon. Indeed, it may well be a thoroughbred and, upon being offered it, you feel you have at last got somewhere. The creature responds immediately to the aids, starts gaily down the lane and out on to the wide open spaces. Reaching a long, level stretch where you have been accustomed to cantering the other creatures in the school string, you do the same. It is only when the animal increases its canter to a gallop that it dawns upon you that it has no brakes. Scattering pedestrians and other

riders from your furious path, you again arrive back in the stable yard earlier than expected. You have the alternative of thinking up another appointment or boldly stating that you cannot hold the brute. Whichever you decide upon, you will be advised to extend the course of lessons because ' your hands aren't right '. This sort of horse is particularly valuable to the stable because it completes an hour's ride in half the time but at the same price.

There is, of course, a type of riding school with perfect horses and perfect instructors for all pupils, and this is the type run by all riding masters and riding mistresses who happen to read this book.

IV

Gymkhanas

THE gymkhana is a fiendish torture of Oriental origin now practised annually in rural Britain in summer. The rites are performed either in blazing hot weather or in pouring rain, usually the latter. The victims sacrificed are parents, dragged out to admire the prowess of their own and other people's offspring, the local landowner, whose turf is battered by tiny hoofs, and villagers, dragged in to stand for hours at the gates taking money or to risk their popularity and necks sorting cars and ponies into some sort of order.

The beneficiaries of the gymkhana are the local good cause, the young riders for whom the occasion is a great opportunity to impress and to get even with some hated rival, the ponies who are able to get even with their riders, and the man who runs the refreshment tent.

Having now learned from the riding school to unlearn all that Uncle George taught you about riding, you feel you are sufficiently accomplished to enter for the classes for older competitors. You will have filled in an imposing entry form to get your own and your pony's name into the programme. This alone is worth an entrance fee, for they will remain there even if you cancel at the last moment and you will be able to show them to your grandchildren one day.

You will probably have entered for the bending race, the egg and spoon, local jumping and the musical chairs —that riot at the end that settles old feuds and starts new ones. You will be on the ground early with your pony in order to get good shelter under the trees from the weather and to have an orgy of soft drinks to steady your nerves. For the first few hours after the start, you will be able to watch the cream of local juvenile horsemanship either being led round the ring or being got away with in the classes for younger riders. These will be won by the youngest child of the famous local horsey family, which every district in England has.

Arguments among parents and committee members as to whether the child is really qualified to have entered because of her age, or her pony because of its height, will set back the programme schedule by some quarter of an hour. Because of this delay, the competitors for the next classes in the ring will have become fed up with waiting and will be missing. When they have been rounded up and herded into the ring, the judges will be missing. Having herded the judges out of the refreshment tent, the programme will continue, now three-quarters of an hour late.

Once the delay has begun, it accumulates, which adds considerably to the fun, as old ladies and the non-horse-minded public, generally, will not have the least idea which class they are watching and will be convinced for the rest of their lives that Working Hunters must always be ridden in fancy dress, and eggs and spoons are always carried in Best Riding Horse classes. The unfortunate person detailed to do the announcing will make frequent attempts to sort this confusion out, but will probably add to it, because he is always being given the wrong results and will have to spend most of his time making corrections and advertising for lost children.

At last the time for your first class, the bending race for the older teen-agers, arrives. A bending race consists of weaving your pony in and out of a long line of poles. You have, of course, practised this in the paddock until your pony is almost hinged in the middle. But the roar of the crowd—those that are not in the beer tent, asleep in their cars, or having a picnic in the far corner of the field—excites the beast and you pass the poles at a gallop, having to dash back to the beginning and start again. Half way down the line it will dawn on you that everyone else has finished, the winner being the eldest daughter of the local horsey family, on a pony that is so used to the job that it instinctively zig-zags at the sight of telegraph poles on a roadside.

You will retire to the refreshment tent and foam with fury and soft drinks, temporarily alarming the local vet. The egg and spoon race has much the same result as the bending race but this time you suspect the winner has made surreptitious use of chewing gum. The Local Jumping class is an event in which most of the spectators will take a keen and anticipatory interest, for there is always an excellent chance that it will provide a good laugh and perhaps a rider or two will even have to be carried off.

It will be just about now that the commentator, hurrying out of the beer tent where he has been seeking information, announces the arrival of a rising young show-jumping starlet who is perfectly entitled to enter as she lives just within the mileage laid down to qualify her as "local". The clanking of silverware from within the horsebox out of which she scrambles reveals that she has been having yet another successful day within the county.

This is somewhat shattering to you. Your pony feels like a cart-horse and, after coping with a brush fence, treats the triple bar as if it were some horror from another world,

Over jumps without their horses

refusing to go within yards of it. Thereafter you retire to the back of the crowd, watching the starlet and noting how it should be done. The fact that three of your acquaintances, including one you loathe, disappear over jumps without their horses cheers you up no end, and you wait

Musical Chairs

with scarcely suppressed excitement for the finale, the Musical Chairs.

This event would have delighted even the savage horsemen of Genghis Khan, for there is much furious riding and sometimes near massacre. You will start off decorously enough, responding to the appeal of the commentator for ' sportsmanship and no rough stuff please '.

As the chairs, which will in fact be boxes, are reduced in number and defeated competitors retire with sickly smiles or thunderous frowns, the remainder begin to lose their inhibitions. If you are in the last half dozen, you may find yourself whooping like an Amazon and going savage to the point of whirling some rival away from her box by the pigtails. Even ponies are apt to join in and bite each other and any legs and arms available. Stewards, removing the boxes, run for their lives and are likely to be galloped into the ground, but no one cares as they won't be wanted after this.

Violent Collision

At last there are only two competitors left—that horrid brunette and yourself. You are told to gallop in opposite directions round the ring in the centre of which is the last box. Faster and faster you go until, like knights in a tourney, you come face to face. There is a crash as you meet in violent collision. As the brunette is carried off, you feel there is much to be said for gymkhanas.

V

Horse Shows

THE big horse shows consist of a lot of horses, even more people, a brass band and a bar with a striped awning under which the most knowledgeable people are to be found, occasionally looking over their shoulders at the horses and at the less knowledgeable people.

You will have gathered from the reference to knowledgeable people that this is where the expert section of this book begins and, having fallen off your horse frequently by now, you can regard yourself as an expert. Let us consider what happens at the biggest horse shows which, curiously enough, are held in the wilds of Shepherd's Bush and North London where the natives regard a live horse with astonishment.

Briefly, much the same thing happens at horse shows as at gymkhanas, only in a more dignified and expensive way. Certainly, most of the horse show competitors bear the scars they won at gymkhanas in their youth, and so do some of the spectators.

The horses are divided into classes, and once upon a time the spectators were too. There are classes for ponies, but instead of being hairy they have been shaved and polished up a bit. Then there are hacks, rudely described

Knowledgeable People

by some hunting people as 'tittuppy-tittuppy' horses, and hunters, offensively described by some hacking people as 'gallopy-gallopy' horses, cobs, which are the sort of horses that would smoke pipes if they were human, hackneys, which are described by some hacking and hunting people, who cannot afford them, as useless luxuries and, of course, show-jumpers which are instantly recognised by everyone who has a T.V. set.

The horses are sorted out into batches of roughly the same shape and size and made to walk, trot, canter and gallop around the ring in front of a few solemn-looking characters in bowler hats. These are the judges and very brave they are because, after some of their decisions, even their best friends won't speak to them.

One of the most important things to do if you are a spectator is to anticipate the judging in order to impress your companions. Here are a few hints. All you need is keen eyesight. Watch the official judges closely, not the horses. If they look scared stiff, or even just peevish, as

Watch the official judges

they ride an animal round the ring, it is a pretty safe bet that that horse will finish well down the list. If they are bucked off it is quite certain.

Do not take any notice of the fact that some judges may smile at and even speak to a competitor as they are helped into the saddle, because judges, as every expert knows, are never influenced by the identity of the rider or owner of a particular horse. What you must watch for is the almost imperceptible sign they give, such as pointing at an animal or beckoning the rider into the centre of the ring. This is the moment when you announce loudly that it was a clear winner from the start, has great depth, magnificent shoulders, beautiful withers, gigantic hocks and so on.

True, you risk being caught out, because some judges rudely point at a horse or competitor with whom they have had an argument, or beckon them in to tell them to get out of the ring, but in this case you swiftly add that you realised at once that the chap ' on top ' (smart slang for ' in the saddle ') was no horseman and was ruining the animal's chances. There is, in fact, only one real danger, and that is that the person sitting in front of you may own the horse.

Show jumping is the most important of the events at a horse show unless you are the owner and/or rider of any other type of horse. There are three chief types of experts on show-jumping, and the T.V.-viewing experts are the most numerous of these. They know the names of all the

Horse show types

horses and riders and also know what they ought to have done and ought not to have done and insist on telling you so whenever they meet you. The only way you can catch them out is by taking them to the show where they may be completely flummoxed by seeing the horses in colour.

The second section of experts consists of the regular show-goers who call out ' good old so-and-so ' from time to time and remark in loud voices that the horse in the ring is just like one they rode in the Brigade show in India and then spend the rest of the competition telling the six rows of spectators in their immediate vicinity how they won.

The third section of experts is a small one consisting of the people who ride the horses, and, of course, these are only important when they show that they know you if you meet them around the ring or sign one of their books for you. It takes a most experienced show-goer to recognise the show-jumping personalities when they are not on their horses, because they often disguise themselves heavily as non-experts. For instance, Miss Blank, who looks radiantly lovely in the saddle, may appear to be a walking mass of windcheaters, pullovers and old hacking jackets at the ringside, and you can't go by her voice because it will be muffled by scarves. You cannot very well grab the bundle and shout ' Congratulations Miss Blank ' into it, because it would be so embarrassing if it turned out to be only a girl groom underneath. There is, however, an infallible rule which will enable you to astonish your friends. Learn to recognise them by their boots.

These fellows and girls are all friendly rivals, because, as every expert knows, there is no other sort of rivalry in show-jumping. If you think you see one of them scowling at another you are quite wrong, unless it is because their caps are giving them a headache or their boots are too tight.

Learn to recognise them by their boots

It is useful, if not absolutely essential, to have abroad competitors at international horse shows, and it is generally recognised in this country that show-jumping has done more for international goodwill than any other form of sport, especially as it is the sport at which we are usually best. The fact that horse sportsmen are better sportsmen than mere foot sportsmen is practically proved by the fact that it is quite a long time since the competitors at a horse show attempted to lynch the judges. There are, after all, more civilised ways of getting even, particularly as horse-show judges can sometimes be persuaded to buy horses.

VI

Advanced Equitation

WHEN it became obvious to expert instructors that too many people were becoming accomplished horsemen and horsewomen, they invented Advanced Equitation to make it all the more difficult again. Advanced Equitation is particularly difficult because no one quite knows what it is, but it can generally be assumed to include the obscurer forms of horsemanship from Advanced Dressage to Advanced Show-Jumping Seats.

Most books on advanced horsemanship are written by abroad cavalry officers in their own language. The books are then translated into English, although this is not always immediately apparent to the reader. Abroad people have always been good at dressage, but British horsemen, being under the impression that the word had something to do with Ruritanian uniforms, considered it was out of place except in musical comedy. In recent years, however, the British have been persuaded that it has something to do with horses, our advanced horsemen have now taken it up, and it is becoming fashionable to pronounce it "dressidge". This is to prove that it is nothing to be afraid of and that not only can we do it, but we can do it in our own language, too.

Ironing your horse's legs straight

We will take a simple example of a typical advanced dressage test to show you how it works. Letters of the alphabet are placed around an arena and you then collect your horse—dressage horses always have to be collected—and make it perform various movements at various paces between those letters. It is usual to enter at a canter, halt in front of the judges and salute. You begin, rather surprisingly, by taking the first track to the right, and we assume that while you are away the judges and spectators play cards or indulge in polite conversation. When you reappear, you have to change reins, the first lot presumably having broken.

You then go off on two tracks which is, of course, extremely difficult, unless you take one track and your horse takes the other. No maps are provided, but if you are lucky enough to meet your horse again you both promptly take a track to the left and, oh bother, you have to change your reins again. (One cannot help feeling that this part of dressage was invented by a saddler.)

Don't go away, we haven't finished yet. You next go for an extended walk and, after a few more tracks to right and left, you go into a positive orgy of ordinary trots, ordinary

canters, extended trots, extended canters, crab-wise movements, half-trots, half-canters and half-passages and then,
just when you are half dead and half dazed, you salute and
walk out. You will spend the next hour or so ironing your
horse's legs straight after the tangle they got into during
the crab-wise movements.

It will be obvious from this that the object of dressage is
to prove the suppleness of the horse, its equipoise and

Dressage in the hunting field

general obedience to its rider. After all, as one expert has written, if a horse will do this for you it will do anything, a view expressed in other words by a famous Master of Hounds who, after watching a dressage display, remarked, ' If a horse did that with me I would hit it over the head.' Yet another authority has said, ' There is probably a messidge in dressidge.'

Mark you, dressage has come to stay, and it will not be long before it spreads to the hunting field. We shall soon see members of the field going sideways and backwards and taking tracks to the left and right and half-trotting and half-cantering all over the place, instead of patiently waiting at covert-side. Come to think of it, it must have spread already.

Another most important part of advanced horsemanship is the Advanced Show-Jumping Seat. This, although another abroad idea, is also now practised with some success by some of our own horsemen and horsewomen, and you

The advanced show-jumping seat

*Mounted policemen still have to use advanced
horsemanship*

will have noticed the object is to take as much weight off
the horse as possible. In fact, the ideal seems to be to leave
the horse altogether as it takes off, rejoining it smartly on
the landing side of the fence. The advanced jumping seat is
sometimes in advance of the saddle, often in advance of
the horse's ears and, in very advanced cases, in advance of
the horse itself.

Advanced horsemanship has been practised for some
time by such advanced horsemen as cavalry officers and
mounted policemen. You have only to mention the subject
and cavalry officers will promptly climb out of their tanks
and dismount from their armoured cars to explain that the
army has known about it all along but has always simply
called it ' schooling the horse '. If you show a willingness to
listen, they may even take you into the Cavalry Club and
explain, with the aid of squadrons of glasses, how the
cavalry used it in battles.

Mounted policemen still have to use advanced horsemanship when they are on their ordinary hoof-beats in the street. They have to know how to go crab-wise at the shortest notice during the traffic rush hours, even to the extent of having to half-disappear down half-passages when pursued by buses.

Of course, mounted policemen look down on horseless carriages. For one thing, it is the only view of them they can get from the back of a horse, and this is another instance where their advanced horsemanship comes in, because, to take a driver's name and address, they have to hang half upside down to see inside the vehicle.

Advanced horsemanship may seem very difficult, but it is possible for every horseman to become an advanced horseman if they manage to become horsemen of advanced age.

VII

Foxhunting

THE secret ambition of anyone who has ever patted a horse without being bitten is to go foxhunting. This is absolutely right and proper and the more people who pat horses without being bitten the better. Foxhunting, say the experts, is behind all horsemanship, and the first time you go foxhunting you will be wise to be behind all the other horsemen.

Lots of people who are sufficiently competent to hunt, because they have paid out quantities of pocket money to riding instructors, are afraid to do so. It is not the fences they fear but the fearsome feudal atmosphere of the hunting field.

Set your fears at rest. Hunting today has gone completely democratic. Ignore members of the Old School who say that makes it more frightening than ever. On the contrary, a hunt today is just one jolly party with everyone riding hither and thither, willy and nilly, and it is now so democratic that even farmers are allowed to join in. Instead of touching their forelocks and muttering under their breaths as people gallop over their crops, which they did when they were tenants of the wicked squires, they are themselves able to gallop all over their own and their

A well galloped-in old farmer

neighbours' crops and even over each other. This they find the greatest fun of all, and nothing is so good for crops as a well galloped-in old farmer. Many of the farmers are even Masters of Hounds which puts them in the embarrassing position of being unable to grumble about the hunt and of having to send themselves home for leaving their own gates open.

Like all experts you will now have, prominently displayed in your bookshelves, works with such titles as *Whither Hunting?*, *Thither Hunting* and *Why Hunting?* Let us hope this chapter will induce you to open some of them.

The Master, who is Head of the Hunt, usually has two or three paid hunt servants. The most important of these is the Huntsman whose job it is to make hounds find foxes

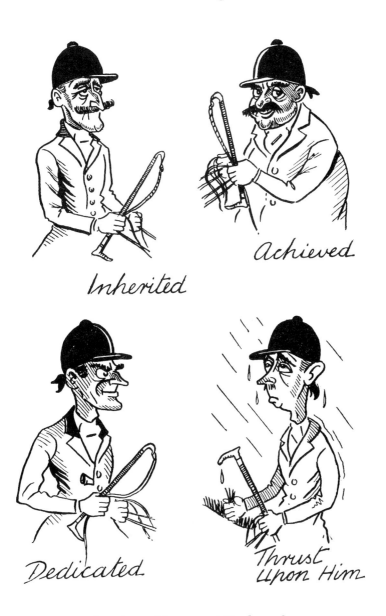

Specimen Masters of Foxhounds

and hunt them in spite of any orders he receives from the Master. Beneath him is the First Whipper-In who has to go to the end of the covert in which hounds and Huntsman are looking for the fox and give a holloa when the fox goes away. The fox usually comes out on the opposite side to the Whipper-In, who is then cursed by the Huntsman, but this doesn't really matter because there is a Second Whipper-In whose duty it is to count hounds and be cursed by the First Whipper-In. Sometimes the Master is also his own Huntsman and this is a good idea because it saves money, arguments and, very often, foxes.

There is not much new to be said about foxes, by the way, except that, to be absolutely up to date, it should be mentioned that they have not died out as a result of a rabbit shortage but merely changed their menu. Learned gentlemen have discovered that they now eat just about everything from old boots to old farm workers but are still not enthusiastic about old boiling fowls left out at night for the purpose. Far from having to tighten their belts, they are still to be found in braces.

Despite the polite democratic spirit of modern hunting, which is particularly noticeable in the queues waiting to jump the gap in the wire ('no, after you'), there are still a few important do's and don'ts the novice must remember. Don't worry unduly about the Master, but do keep out of his way when you are hunting, just in case he is still a bit old-fashioned, and do be nice to him when you meet him without a horse. He might want to buy one.

Do keep a good look-out for the Hunt Secretary, who will certainly be keeping a good look-out for you, particularly after you have been out a few times without any money on you.

Don't jump on anyone you don't know and don't fall off in front of anyone you don't like. If anyone else falls off, do catch their horse—it may be much better than yours.

Do raise your hat to everyone at the meet except, of course, the previously mentioned Hunt Secretary who would, in response, promptly hold his out.

Some M's F.H. complain that too many people who go hunting today are not sufficiently interested in hounds. This is certainly a point. You should know each one by name and be nice to it in case one day you jump into the middle of the pack and fall off. Your fate will then depend upon whether the Master or a hound to which you have been nice gets hold of you first.

A most important section of the modern hunting field is the group of jovial supporters known as the 'Car Brigade'. These are a great help to the Master, because they can always tell him where the fox was going when they got there and prevented it. Sometimes, if you are among the last riders in the field, they will help your horse

Sit on their radiators for a mile or two

by allowing it to sit on their radiators for a mile or two.
If the fox you are pursuing is one of the modern sort that
lives in a kale field and runs in short circles (the theory
that modern foxes have shorter legs on one side than the
other is discounted by the experts), you will again catch up
with the Car Brigade and be able to rest your horse's front
legs on the boot of the last vehicle.

Never be rude to members of the Car Brigade. You
might want a lift when you fall off and, anyway, where
would we be without 'em? Galloping vulgarly straight up
the tarmac probably, instead of sneaking past them along
the ditch like gentlemen.

It is well known that hunts have not got any money these
days, and one of the few things that keeps hunting going
is the annual Point-to-Point. Contrary to the ideas of the
ill-informed and general appearances, these are not just

steeplechases in which the entries are all race horses. They are races over a course with as natural hunting fences as possible in which only bona fide hunters take part. All these horses have to qualify for a certificate from the Master to the effect that they have been regularly and fairly hunted. If you keep to the rear of the field, you can see them doing it, particularly at the opening meet. Point-to-Point horses, being well bred, are always liable to make an impression, and they will make it on you if you get too close.

Yes, you must certainly go hunting, especially at the opening meet or on Boxing Day when there are Press photographers about. After all, once you have got the proof you needn't go out again.

(In chapters about hunting, it is customary to include a glossary of 'Common Expressions in the Hunting Field' but you will not find one here because they are not to be encouraged.)

VIII

Horse Trials

SOMEONE, probably a motorist, once said that horsemen enjoyed horsemanship because it was apt to be so painful. This is probably also the horse's point of view and, to make sure that neither horse nor rider become complacent, a new horse sport has been thought up since the war, called, appropriately enough, Horse Trials.

Each trial is split up into three phases. They are dressage, speed and endurance, and show-jumping. The object of the trials is to test ' the complete horse and horseman ' which automatically eliminates any three-legged horses and any horseman who is not absolutely sane. Each horse and rider has to do the three phases to prove that they are supple, fast, endurable and still able to stand up at the end.

The most important horse trials, like the most important human trials, go on for three days. On the dressage day the dressage enthusiasts sit around on bales of straw or on the roofs of their cars, trying to avoid, not too strenuously, being photographed by photographers from glossy magazines. At one end of the dressage arena, in a tent, are the judges who have to be not only dressage experts but also mathematicians, because they have to add up and subtract the points dropped by the horses during their performances.

But you already know all about dressage and it is the next phase, the speed-and-endurance test, that is the most interesting. It somewhat resembles foxhunting without the encumbrance of Masters, Huntsmen and hounds, but also without the gaps in the fences and the foot people to open the gates that adds so greatly to the enjoyment of many hunting people today.

There is also the putting-off presence of hundreds of spectators standing around with their mouths open waiting for the riders to be put off. The speed-and-endurance phase attracts large crowds of unknowledgeable people as well as knowledgeable people. It is particularly popular with the unknowledgeable people because they can join in on foot, one of their favourite games being to clog up the narrow tracks just before a galloping horse is due and to play 'last across' in front of a particularly nasty fence to make things more interesting for the competitors.

A suggested new trials obstacle

There is usually a notice in the programmes asking people not to bring their dogs with them. This is regarded as screamingly funny by the unknowledgeable people, who promptly bring lots of little dogs with them to add to the horse trials.

It has even been suggested that the organisers should introduce a pack of little dogs as one of the obstacles, but this is naturally opposed by little dog-owners who point out that it is much more fun for the little dogs if they are used individually.

The spectators are mobile

This phase of the trials includes long rides along tracks (not to be confused with the dressage tracks) and a gallop over a steeplechase course as well as over a large number of assorted, nasty, cross-country obstacles such as banks, quarries, ponds, ditches, gates, hay-racks, stewards, spectators and the afore-mentioned little dogs.

This is one of the few sporting events at which the spectators are mobile. They are allowed to move about in flocks from jump to jump, inspecting them and remarking, as

The Quarry

Drop Fence

Typical trials obstacles

they sit on their shooting sticks, that any good hunter could do that and that they would probably have been competing themselves if their horses weren't lame.

It must be mentioned that, as the trials usually take place when foxes are nesting and consequently there is a gentlemen's agreement not to annoy them, you will find whole packs of hunting folk feathering around the trials grounds, giving tongue whenever they meet each other. The trials, therefore, are among the best places at which to pick up intelligent snatches of hunting conversation which you can use yourself later on.

Separated from his horse

The more important horse trials, like the more important horse shows, are extremely good for international sportsmanship. For one thing, a number of international experts have to get together first to agree about the rules, and this in itself, these days, is a considerable international achievement. Just to quote one example, it has been internationally agreed that the definition of a fall from a horse is when a rider is ' separated from his horse, which has not fallen, in such a way as to necessitate remounting or vaulting into the saddle '. What could be fairer than that?

The third phase of the trials consists of show-jumping, and this is particularly trying to the spectators who will have discovered by now that their mathematics are not what they were and will have become quite confused by the system of scoring in which phases and bonuses and penalties and speeds at yards or metres per minute are all added up and subtracted. For one thing, they have to remember that ' a penalty of a quarter of a point is incurred for each commenced second taken in excess of time allowed up to the time limit, after which competitors are eliminated, and that the time limit is twice the time allowed '.

Some people find these calculations require even more endurance than taking part in the trials and consequently turn up on a horse the next year.

IX

The Horse in Harness

Jolly Christmas coaching scene

PROBABLY because it had long been in the habit of standing about in the wide open draughty spaces, the horse was a draught animal from very early days. Man, tired of carrying girl friends and other shopping about on his back, soon learned to make the horse drag his baggage along in a cart.

The earliest form of cart consisted of a couple of poles tied together at the end farthest from the horse with skins placed across them to carry the baggage. Then one day, man, messing about with some branches of trees, discovered they could be used as wheels and, by inventing wheeled transport, was responsible for all the waiting about we suffer today.

After a time proper carts were invented but, as no-one, except the Romans, thought much of road-building, and even the Roman roads became rather rough after the Romans were demobilised, people in carts in ancient Britain had rather rough rides. This didn't really matter very much as it was only the rougher type of people who had the rough rides, the more intelligent and bolder types having already learned to ride on horses' backs by this time.

In due course, someone did get around to making more and better roads of a sort, and waggons and heavy coaches were built to carry more parcels and people. But the roads were still rather bumpy and coach passengers spent as much time in the air as on their seats, particularly the out-side passengers who were often much more outside than they meant to be.

Now everything in connection with horses has a hey-day, and one of the hey-days most frequently referred to by those of us who write about horses is the hey-day of coaching. This is undoubtedly one of the most important of all because it has provided us with the jolliest Christmas cards and calendars and the jolliest glossy Christmas magazines.

The coaching hey-day began when much better roads were invented. This made it possible to have much faster coaches with faster horses and often faster passengers as well. The mail coaches were the fastest of the lot, and it is customary for sophisticated coaching people to talk about 'the mails' when discussing the old days. This is very confusing for non-coaching people, who imagine that references to ' the day the old Exeter mail was found in a ditch ' are callous comments about the habits of an oldest inhabitant of Devonshire.

One of the most delightful things about coaching is that it was responsible for jolly old coaching inns with jolly old landlords and jolly old ostlers. Many of these jolly old inns still exist, and you can tell them by the notices which say so outside and by the fact that they have high archways leading into the yard where the coachmen swopped horses when they had had enough of their own. The inns with high archways were the most popular because low archways were inclined to give the outside passengers headaches.

One of the great things about coaching is that it is always being revived by jolly amateur coachmen, and

Pull the right reins at the right time

there has been at least one revival since the war, thanks largely to the efforts of a poor working farmer or two and some refreshment gentlemen.

People who watch coaches being driven at shows today are apt to think that coach-driving is easy. On the contrary, it is not even easy to climb up on to a coach, and one of the things that makes jolly amateur coachmen of today jollier than ever is to invite non-coaching people to get up on to the top of their coaches and then watch them trying to do so. To a coaching person, one of the jolliest things to be seen is a non-coaching person hanging upside down like a bat by one foot.

Be careful about using the whip

Driving four horses is even more difficult than climbing on to a coach. Each horse has to have reins, and you have to be careful to pull the right reins at the right time or you get in an awful muddle. You must also be careful about using the whip or else you will make the passenger on the box seat choke with laughter, or perhaps just choke.

At the back of the coach there was and still is, if he hasn't fallen off, a man with a long trumpet who plays tunes from time to time. He always wears a top hat, and it is also good taste for male passengers to wear top hats, this being a relic of the old days when top hats were used to measure the clearance between heads and archways.

In addition to faster coaches, better roads encouraged other faster vehicles such as the curricle which had two wheels and two horses, the cabiolet which had one horse and two people, the hansom cab which had one horse and two people inside with another nosey old person on the roof listening in, the gig which often contained two giggling people, the tub cart which would hold several tubby people and the float in which farmers floated back from the inn. There were also post-chaises which were useful if you had to chase the post.

Apart from the coaching classes, one of the most interesting popular survivals of the driving age at horse shows

Hackney groom going for a drink

today is the hackney which is available in two sizes, horse size and pony size, and is rather expensive in both. It goes round the ring on springs, just missing its nose with its knees and drawing hackney people on tiny hackney carts while the band plays old hackney carriage-horse music. You can nearly always tell hackney people by the way they walk, and even old hackney grooms often bang their noses with their knees when hurrying for a drink.

X

Social Occasions

THE horse is by nature an extremely sociable creature as you will have discovered when trying to subtract one from a number. Humans are also sociable by nature, and it follows that humans associated with horses are even more sociable than foot humans.

Horse people have any amount of social occasions, but before you take part in them you must learn that it is not the thing for those who like horses to admit in public that they like social occasions as well.

The traditionally correct attitude is to remark that you loathe getting into evening dress and would far rather be putting on your riding boots than dancing shoes, adding that the music of hounds is far sweeter than the music of somebody or other's beastly dance band. You then allow yourself to be dragged, protesting, to all the social occasions for which you manage to wangle an invitation.

The Greeks and the Romans, according to the social magazines of the day, were madly social at horse and chariot races and, wearing their best togas and other fashionable garments, laughed madly and sociably whenever anyone fell out of his chariot, particularly if he did so in front of another chariot.

In Mediaeval times the tournaments were the most important social events, and the spectators laughed mediaevally together whenever a knight received a battle-axe in the gizzard.

In Tudor and Stuart times there were many merry horseback, hawking, and hunting parties and this, with the exception of a short break during Cromwellian times when the 'No Hawkers' signs were put up, continued until foxhunting got going thoroughly and special social fox-hunting events were invented. At all these social occasions connected with the horse everyone talked horse to prove that they knew about them.

There is really no point in knowing about horses unless you let everyone else know that you know and the best opportunity of doing so is at a social event attended by the horse-minded.

The Hunt Ball is the most favourable occasion of all because it is quite correct to talk loudly about the horse there and, in fact, rather incorrect not to do so. If you are prepared to shout yourself hoarse you stand a reasonable chance of making yourself overhead by people at the next table.

You can always tell you are at a hunt ball by the old fox masks around the walls, the old waiter masks around the buffet and the old hunting masks worn by the old hunting people. Another clue is that there will be a number of people present in hunt evening dress whom you do not remember ever having seen out hunting.

The question of dress is particularly important if you are a girl because it is incorrect to wear red as it will clash with the hunting pink. Curiously enough, it does not matter if the men's faces clash with their own pink coats although this clash is often the worst of all. On the contrary, it is rather bad form to have a pink coat and a white

Hunting people not enjoying Hunt Ball

face. Men should wear tails, and this is about the only hunting occasion on which it is permitted to call tails by that name instead of brushes or sterns.

Hunt balls always start long after people ought to be in bed and go on until long after they ought to have got up. It is traditional to go hunting later the same day and even more traditional to appear to be hearty and not hunting on a hangover. Hunt balls are particularly joyful occasions for the hunt secretary, who goes to ground behind a potted palm to count up the dancers in couples and multiply by guineas.

Race meetings, including Point-to-Points, constitute another highly important section of social occasions connected with the horse. Unlike hunt balls, race meetings do not require any real knowledge of the horse. It is merely

Ladies Race

advisable to be able to tell a mounted police horse from a race-horse at a glance. Another point about race meetings, the most social of which are held in the rain, is that you will have practically nothing to do with the horses at all, and the only dangerous part of the race course is the area where there are men with loud voices standing on boxes and doing sums on blackboards. If you get too close to one of them you are likely to get much more hurt than if you get too close to a horse. You will also learn quite a lot of useful horse-talk if you stand close to a fence during a Point-to-Point race.

Another highly social occasion is a polo match although

this is not always so highly social as it once was because it is now becoming popular again with foot people, who don't understand it, as well as with horse people, who do but can't afford to play. It is an extremely complicated game full of chukkas and polo sticks, a hard ball and tanned Naval and Military-looking men who occasionally exchange greetings when they meet on the field. It doesn't matter if you don't understand it so long as you don't say so and do talk horse now and again. The thing to remember is that instead of using ordinary horse small-talk you should use slightly smaller horse-talk because the horses are usually slightly smaller too.

Special shows of special breed societies like Arabs and Native Ponies are often particularly social because special breeds are often bred by special lady breeders. At these, therefore, you need special horse-talk to prove that you not only know about horses but about special horses as

Exchange greetings when they meet

*A farrier is particularly good at
technical horse-talk*

well. You must also remember to be as social as possible with your farrier because farriers are particularly good at technical horse-talk.

Nowadays there are a large number of riding clubs throughout the country, and these are extremely social as well as horsey because they have film shows, lectures, dances and cocktail parties as well as other trials, and therefore they are about the best places at which to practice talking horse.

Once you have learned, you will go on talking horse all your life until a golfer or an angler or a motorist hits you over the head with a club, a fish or a spanner, because people in these categories are particularly dangerous to horsemen as they have their own special talk and hate listening to any other talk.

XI

The Horse in Literature and in Show Business

Has it occurred to you that if it were not for horse journalists you would know even less about the horse than you do now? No? Then the sooner you realise it the better, for even horse journalists must live—at least, that is their own considered opinion.

One of the first horse journalists was Xenophon who wrote in Greek his famous manual, cavalry officers for the use of. Not only did he write all there was to be written about the horse, but he also gave all other cavalry officers throughout the ages the idea of doing the same thing. The ones that are left are still doing it, sometimes apparently in Greek and sometimes in plain horse-soldier language.

It will become clear as you peruse horse literature that horse journalists, horse poets and even ordinary horse reporters are particularly fond of a special breed of horse which can be traced back to the famous Hobby Horse which was, of course, by Cliché out of Pot-Boiler. It has so far been found quite impossible to wipe out this line and, on the contrary, it is at present very much in favour.

Horses were both ridden about and written about by Roman journalists like Julius Caesar, mediaeval journalists like Chaucer, Elizabethan journalists like Shakespeare and any amount of nineteenth-century journalists like Nimrod and Surtees. Shakespeare has written many flattering things about horses and was obviously very fond of them or there wouldn't be so many in his films. On the other hand, he could not have been thoroughly horse-minded for he makes one character say ' He doth nothing but talk of his horse ', as if it were something to complain about.

In addition to horse journalists there have been, and still are, quite a number of horse poets who write frightfully hearty horse poetry all about flashes of scarlet and thundering hoofs and tantivies and things, and sometimes get them published in horse magazines and horse newspapers.

You can usually tell horse journalists because they stand about wearing horsey hats, fingering their moustaches and talking horse talk to very important horse people at horse shows and horse races. Some hunting journalists can sometimes be seen hunting and at important horse trials like

Horse journalists at Horse Trials

Bred for long screens

Badminton the more important ones can even be seen furiously galloping about making notes which they furiously phone up to their newspapers where non-horse minded journalists translate their words into non-horse language that can be understood by all readers except those who know about horses.

Since moving pictures were invented, horses have been earning extra corn money in films, and the ones that earn the most are those that stand on their hind legs whenever the hero gets on their backs. There are also lots of extra horses, who dash about in clouds of dust and turn somersaults in cavalry charges, and also extra wide horses on which villains can carry off heroines and extra long horses especially bred for the modern long screens.

When film horses retire from galloping about, they sometimes get jobs on the stage in horse operas, standing about with their eyes closed while actors and actresses sit on their backs and sing. Then there is the highly specialised branch of horse acting in circuses which is done by circular horses which go round and round in circles.

One of the most modern professional horses is the B.B.C. horse which performs on sound programmes only. You can always tell it is a horse because it makes a noise like coconuts, neighs a little and is always weighed down with pots and pans that make clanking noises to represent harness. It has much more important colleagues, the T.V. horses, who do a tremendous amount of good showing

Horses who write their own books

people round their country homes and generally letting people who live in towns see that horses are really quite ordinary people like themselves.

Most important of all are the horses who write their own books. These are known in the profession as hackwriters although most of them are really just little whimsey ponies, as you will find out if you ever read their works. Few people, except publishers, realise that at this very moment all over the country all sorts of horses are sitting down on piles of straw in horse boxes and pony boxes and shelters in fields, putting their horse lives down on paper and trying to decide whether to have a happy ending or not. Lots of people think horse authors writing their autobiographies just ought to have an ending, not caring very much whether it is happy or not.

If you are a horse or pony thinking of writing a book there are a few things you must remember. Firstly you

The cult of the Horsey-Worsey

must think back and recall where you spent your foalhood —a moor or a sunny meadow is the usual place—and then you must describe your Mum who must be gentle and kind because no successful horse author ever had a Mum who was horrid and kicked her or him around. Then you must get yourself sold and get yourself broken in and then have a kind owner who must have to sell you or lose you or something. After this you must have a perfectly beastly time for a bit, and then your first owner must find you again and it probably serves him or her jolly well right.

Since the rediscovery of the horse in a big way by horse-journalists, horse poets and horses themselves, there have been signs of a horse revival to the extent of a positively Horsey-Worsey Cult, with fox masks and coach horns and post horns and hunting horns and horse shoes and horse brasses plastered all over the walls of horsey-worsey inns run by horsey-worsey landlords and frequented by horsey-worsey customers. But we won't go into that—or them—more than we have to do.

XII

How to get rid of your Horse

PERHAPS the most difficult thing connected with horses is getting rid of them. Now that you know all about horses and your own has several times got rid of you, you will undoubtedly want to get rid of it. The most sensible way of getting rid of your horse is selling it at a profit. It is certainly not much use trying to give it away, particularly in your own county, because you will find that everyone knows all about it and won't even look it in the mouth.

You may at first think that the best thing to do is to get into touch with the hairy old dealer who sold you the animal. This, however, will prove pointless because the dealer will either have shaved by now and consequently be unrecognisable, or will find a lot of things about the horse that have deteriorated since you have had it, such as its wind, its manners, its vices and even its pedigree.

The wisest plan is to advertise in special horse newspapers which are read only by horses and hounds and horse people and hound people. Before you do this you must be familiar with some of the correct horse selling terms and what they mean. The following are some useful definitions:

IDEAL FOR A BEGINNER: The horse doesn't know anything either, so they might as well learn together.

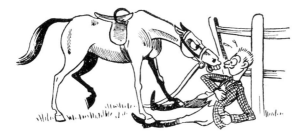

Easy to catch

SUITS ELDERLY GENTLEMAN: At his age nobody much minds what happens to him anyway.

HAS BEEN REGULARLY HUNTED: Particularly by the owner who has had to chase it all over the county.

QUIET WITH HOUNDS: A valuable animal because it can take a sly kick at them without neighing with laughter and attracting the attention of the Master.

Lives out

EASY TO CATCH: Stands over the rider whenever it has bucked him off.

SOUND: Sings, whistles and roars.

WILL JUMP ANYTHING: Especially out of its field, over its rider, horse show judges and spectators.

LIVES OUT: Spends most of its time in other people's fields and gardens.

LIVES IN: Confirmed cadger; difficult to keep it out of the kitchen.

GOOD DOER: Will do anybody it can lay its teeth on.

Almost any horse can be placed in one of these categories and all you have to do, once the advertisement has been paid for, is to retire, like a spider into your web, and wait for your first victim. In due course one will arrive and ask to see the creature. The horse, not expecting visitors, will be looking its worst, not even having done its hair.

Good doer

The victim begins to examine it, going first to the front end to look it in the eye. This he finds difficult because the eye keeps rolling. Behind the victim's back you try frantically to put the horse in a pleasant mood by indicating that you have some sugar. The animal, which appears even dumber than usual this morning, suddenly gets the idea, takes a step forward on to the victim's toe and butts him over with its great ugly head.

Removing the horse's other hoof from the victim's face you extract him from beneath the animal and remark that it is amazingly gentle with children.

Now comes the awkward moment when the victim will drift around to the rear end, unaware of the awful danger to which he is exposing himself. You try hard to keep him otherwise occupied but he insists on a close inspection of the hind legs.

You retrieve the victim from the spot, fifty yards away, to which he has suddenly and unwillingly gone, dust him down and ask him if he would like to ride the beast. Although by now he is looking doubtful and beginning to mutter that he is not sure that it is quite what he wanted, he plucks up courage and says, yes, he would like to get on its back.

A saddle is fetched, up gets the prospective purchaser and so does the horse. You remark that he is a bit keen, hasn't been out much recently, too much corn, etc. Horse and rider go round the field and when the horse comes back you light a cigarette and wait for the rider. The thing to do now is to imply that he voluntarily dismounted, and you must do this quickly, before he has time to make any comments himself. You will probably have the initiative anyway, because his mouth will most likely be full of turf.

When he can speak again, he will do one of two things. He will either go off in his car without speaking at all, or buy the brute for a quarter of the price you paid for it.

Some people advocate leaving the stable door or paddock gate open as a means of getting rid of a horse and shutting them smartly when the animal has gone.

This only works when you don't want to get rid of your horse. It is surprising how a really large horse that gets out against your wishes can walk along main roads, through towns and farmyards, remaining invisible, whereas a horse you desperately want to lose is spotted at once by the local constabulary or even by small children, and brought back before it has had time to go a few hundred yards. Even worse, some horses hang around just outside the door or gate, refusing to go away at all, and so you have to let them in again.

Lending a horse you don't want doesn't work either. You will soon find that people will not return books or lawn mowers but never forget to return a horse, particularly at the end of the summer. This is probably because books and lawn mowers don't eat. No, it is absolutely useless going all Shakespearean and shouting 'Farewell the neighing steed!' because it is ten-to-one the brute will soon be neighing away again on your premises, the middle of the night being a favourite time.

When one really considers the whole subject of human relationship with horses one becomes aware that, after all, the initiative is mostly with the horse and that it is the horse who gets rid of the rider when he decides to do so. And that, now we come to think of it, is the main theme of this book.